Between the Silences

Diane Buchanan

Frontenac House
Calgary, Alberta

Book and cover design: Epix Design
Author photo: Beryl Shoults

Library and Archives Canada Cataloguing in Publication

Buchanan, Diane B.
        Between the silences / Diane Buchanan.

Poems.
ISBN 0-9732380-8-9

        1.Title.
PS8553.U43333B48 2005 C811'.6 C2005-900337-5

We acknowledge the support of the Canada Council for the Arts
which last year invested $20.3 million in writing and publishing
throughout Canada. We also acknowledge the support of The
Alberta Foundation for the Arts.

Canada Council Conseil des Arts
for the Arts   du Canada

Printed and bound in Canada
Published by Frontenac House Ltd.
1138 Frontenac Avenue S.W.
Calgary, Alberta, T2T 1B6, Canada
Tel: 403-245-2491   Fax: 403-245-2380
editor@frontenachouse.com   www.frontenachouse.com

1 2 3 4 5 6 7 8 9 09 08 07 06 05

Between the Silences invites us to sit in the back row of Family and Youth Court, where important decisions are made every day – decisions that can affect our children, our families, our friends, our neighbours, our communities. The fortunate among us will never be inside a courthouse. But Diane Buchanan takes us there with her poetry. Writing with the heart of a woman who is both nurse and mother, she uses poetry not to lull us but to wake us up. In a series of word snapshots and evocative portraits she creates a collage of images both thought-provoking and heartrending. *Between the Silences* reveals that strange and poignant world on the other side of the courthouse door.

Also by Diane Buchanan:

Ask Her Anything

For Donald
– my inspiration

Acknowledgements

I wrote the poem *Inferno* after reading Paul Cohan's poem *Aspen Tree*. *Outside Her Window* was inspired by a painting by Patrick Doyle and *Marching Orders* is a found poem taken from *A Probation Order*.

I am indebted to Shirley Serviss, teacher, mentor and friend for her critical reading and judicious comments and to Patrick Lane for encouraging me to "keep writing those courthouse poems."

Many thanks to my other teachers for generously sharing their expertise, particularly: Lorna Crozier, Eunice Scarfe, Betsy Warland and Sheri-D Wilson.

My appreciation extends to all of the wonderful women in my writing groups for their suggestions and their support.

I am grateful always, to my daughters, Ruth, Susan, Meagan, Colleen and my grandson Matthew for sharing their lives with me.

Finally I want to thank the Provincial Court Judges of the Edmonton Family and Youth Court Division for making me feel so welcome in their courtrooms.

The poem *The Judge's Robe* appeared in the *Provincial Judges' Journal*, Winter 2004 issue.

Contents

BETWEEN THE SILENCES

1A Sir Winston Churchill Square

The courthouse
lives   here
    an intimidating body
       with two mouths
facing west and east
      two heads
south and north
inside
      three arteries
carry public, prisoner, judge
             separately.

The courtroom
      is where they meet,
the courtroom,
      windowless, pictureless,
colourless,
the courtroom
      throbs,
the courtroom
      is where the heart sits.

YOUTH COURT

In Youth Docket Court

9:30 a.m. No judge
in this perspiring courtroom,
just a muted buzz amid nervous shuffling
of paper and feet, lawyers and youth,
welfare workers, the occasional parent.
At the front, attorneys chat with each other,
throw legalese around like Frisbees.
Two policemen, elbows on holsters,
pretend to relax, while their eyes rove,
always on duty. The air is muggy
with tension. A girl fingers
her orange spiked hair, three boys
behind snicker and bump. A tattooed teen
in camouflage and army boots turns around
and growls. A young man in shackles
is escorted through the courtroom. The buzzing
settles to a quiet hum. A gowned clerk instructs
all cell phones and pagers off,
announces:

Mics are live.

The heavy oak door at the front
of the courtroom swings open,

Order in court.
All rise.

The judge flows in
black robes swishing,
takes a seat on the podium.

Court is in session.
Please be seated…

*

A young man enters
the prisoner's box, hands
cuffed behind his back.
He looks over
at the spectators
searching
hopefully
for just one
familiar face.

When none appear,
his face
hardens
into cruel resolve.

*

A girl in high boots
and miniskirt is called
before the judge.
She stands –
the lawyers talk,
the judge talks,
and she is dismissed.

Nobody really looks,
nobody really sees,
nobody asks   her.

She becomes –
        nobody.

*

A suit and tie
wheeling a particularly wide
and important briefcase
bristles through the door
and bows
to the judge before
taking a seat. Later
another one turns to bow
before leaving. The young people
feel no need
to bow, nobody
notices them anyway.

*

Her jeans rest on her hips
just below tattoo and thong.
She takes the stand, pleads
guilty to threatening bodily harm,
bullying
three younger girls who now sit
in the back row
of the courtroom.

At the court's direction she turns
and apologizes,
with her mouth –
her eyes
remain
defiant.

*

A fourteen-year-old boy
with dark skin and bowl-cut hair
in custody for break and enter
doesn't know where
his parents are, hasn't seen them
in years, thinks his father could be
in Edmonton, doesn't know anything
about his mother.

*

A fifteen-year-old girl from Tunisia
dwarfs the tiny scarfed woman at her side
as she tells the judge about this woman,
her mother, her language difficulties.
The girl is charged with ignoring curfew.
Her father forbids her
to see her boyfriend,
punishes her
when she disobeys.
The girl rebels,
runs from the fetters of east
into the arms of the west,
then, afraid to return
is caught
in a game
of cultural tug-of-war.

*

Six teenage boys lounge
outside the courtroom
cocky and confident now
they've appeared,
boast they lied,
got off easy,
think they've got it all
figured out.

*

She's seventeen, plays
hide and seek
with a toddler
in the hallway until
it's her turn
to plead
guilty to shop-lifting.
Explains her failure
to appear before. She fled
from her father,
played her own game
of hide and seek.
Now that he's in jail
she promises
to pay the fine,
do community service hours,
look after her own crying child
who is already knocking
at the courtroom door.

*

Standing in the prisoner's box,
his bright freckled face
framed by tousled red hair
his slender body draped
in dark institutional sweats,
he holds his hands behind his back
as if in handcuffs, seems
quite comfortable as he listens
to the prosecutor read his record.
Twenty-two convictions
in the last four years. He's used
the court like a revolving door.
Sixteen now, a small town boy,
he tells the court his crime
was coming back to the city
to see his girlfriend, ignores
the fact that he stole a car,
the neighbour's purse. Now,
he says he's willing to pay a fine,
go back home, get a job, report to the RCMP,
says he's willing to toe the line –
                        at least until next time.

*

She won't look at the judge,
stands sideways, tugs at her jeans,
her sweater until there is only
an inch of skin showing between.
Crossing her arms, she glares
at the toe of her running shoe
punching the courtroom carpet
as the charges against her are read:
robbery, assault, intoxication,
alcohol level over 0.2 percent.

When her mother asks
for counselling this fourteen-year-old
shakes her head to protest, mumbles,
I don't have no problem.

*

A policeman escorts a juvenile
into the prisoner's box. His mother
takes the stand, states
she's willing to try –
again –
to take him home, to keep him
out of trouble.

The boy tells the judge this time
he will not disappoint
the court. This time he will
stay off drugs, finish school.
His mother believes
the week in jail has been a lesson,
believes he really wants to change.

The court wants to believe
him too, releases him –
once more –
into his mother's care.

A caring mother,
is a formidable force.
But then again –
so is crystal meth.

*

At the lawyer's prodding
this small boy pushes back
the black hood of his sweatshirt,
removes the toque underneath
and runs nervous fingers through his
rumpled brown hair bypassing
a particularly unruly piece
at the crown. When called
he comes forward to plead
guilty to shoplifting from Zellers.
Says he took some silly putty
and a box of licorice glossettes.
The judge glares at him through
glasses perched low on his nose,
scolds him for this crime then,
possibly remembering being young
once too, sends him home
with only a reprimand.

Young Offenders

There seems to be
no common denominator
for young offenders. They come
in both genders, all colours,
races, social classes. They come
alone or accompanied. They come
cocky, humble or scared. They come
washed and unwashed, tattooed,
pierced and battle scarred. They come
hungry or well fed, in ragged jeans,
leather jackets, mini skirts,
sometimes even freshly ironed pants.
Nothing in common except
they are under eighteen
and they've been caught
doing whatever it was
that they did or —
didn't do.

Prognosis

I cannot breathe. The courtroom is so full of pain.
It presses into me. A cancerous crime
has sapped strength, stolen joy. Never benign
this sexual abuse has metastasized, randomly laid blame,

invaded lives, divided families, intensified,
until it has turned on itself. The accused, just sixteen,
his actions so malignant, the recriminations so extreme,
he sees his life as worthless, wants to die.

And where is the analgesic for the victim five years old?
No sedation will help her forget, not even the sharpest
scalpel can cut out this tumor, no drug will hold,

no punishment can stop its lethal spread.
No lawyer, no court, no judge can reverse. Incest,
the deed has won. Innocence is already dead.

Show and Tell

Five-year-olds
should be in kindergarten,
not some courtroom,
riding a rocking horse,
not lifted into the witness stand,
singing nursery rhymes,
not answering questions about their private parts,
playing with toys, not a microphone,
seeing Santa Claus, not a judge.
Five-year-olds should be showing off
their new trikes to friends, not pointing
to the site of the bad touch.

Local child porn case to start Monday

–newspaper headline: Victoria, Nov. 28/03

An international sting operation …
arrested 12 people in 15 countries.
    A young man sits alone doing homework,
    the only light his computer screen
    full of facts. He leans back, sighs, shifts
    his fleshy body awkwardly to close the door,
    shutting out his family watching television upstairs.

Technology can deliver images
anywhere in the world in seconds.
    One click and another and another,
    he forgets everything; teachers,
    taunting peers, parents, his body, his hands,
    his eyes seeing what he should never see,
    doing what comes unnaturally.

The internet has brought
the global community to our backyards.
    But backyards are where the skating rinks are,
    backyards are fenced and safe, backyards
    are where our children play, are where
    this young man will head
    when his screen goes dark.

The Haunting

There are ghosts in court today.
Ghosts of bullied victims past.
The courtroom shivers with their swirling.
The odour of their fear has haunted
the defendant for some time now.
Fourteen when his peers first began
to threaten and harass. A year older
when that fear led him to arm himself.

Those ghosts hover nearby
as he takes the witness stand,
a pretty boy with gelled bleached hair,
dressed meticulously in black.
He tells the judge about that day
in the gymnasium, the day
those same boys picked a fight
while the whole class cheered, the day
his fear was so severe he grabbed
the lock and chain from his gym bag
and swung it around until
a teacher interfered, called the police.
He was charged with possession
of a weapon with intent to injure.

Today he's found guilty –
because, of course, by law he is,
although *mitigating circumstances*
allow the penalty to be less severe.
As he stands for sentencing
he hears he's free to go, to unarm himself,
do community service hours,
but it will be much harder to turn off
that fear, lay to rest those victims
of bullying past, leave their ghosts
at the courtroom door.

Trickster

At the trial, an unruly cowlick points
pieces of her short hair heavenward
as she sits perched on the edge
of the chair, feet swinging freely,
too short to reach the floor,
her cupid lips pursed
into a plaintive pout
below naïve, brown eyes.

Another ward of the government,
she lives in a group home,
flashed a knife, robbed the woman
who looked after her.
Only thirteen,

she's been here before,
another assault. She sniffs,
wipes her nose with the sleeve
of her oversized sweatshirt.
All innocence until
she turns to wink at the three boys
sprawled in the back row
with the cunning
of a coyote.

The Professional

He prides himself on his expertise,
specializes in stealing cars,
carries tools on a belt at his waist
holstered like guns, ready for the draw.

Ready for the draw in this courtroom now,
he stands in the prisoners box,
hands cuffed behind his back,
pleads guilty to the charges.

Guilty to the charges of stealing a '97 Pontiac.
Guilty to driving without a license.
Guilty to breaking curfew.
Guilty to having done it before.

Having done it before, now, what to do?
This boy's too young for jail, too old for Tonka toys.
Yet, he's proud of his specialization,
considers himself a professional in his field.

A professional in his field though not yet fourteen.
First tasted booze through his placental cord,
can't read or write, differentiate right from wrong,
he doesn't have a home. No one wants him anymore.

No one wants him anymore the lawyers say.
He stands on tiptoes to peek over the railing,
sniffs loudly then swipes his nose against his upper arm,
looks at the judge with hostile eyes that say it all.

Eyes that say it all, say, help me,
say, hate me, say, like me, say, try me,
say, save me, say, you can't,
say, it's not too late.

Semantics

Her friends pled guilty,
yet she clings to her innocence
like a rock climber frantically seeking
a lost toe hold. On the witness stand
she turtles into hoodie and parka
says she didn't do anything wrong
even though she agreed to help *jack*
a women outside the LRT,
take her Discman, her sweater,
her shoes. Says that *jack*
is not the same as *rob*, not the same
as *theft*. She only asked
for bus tickets, it wasn't her
who hit the woman – twice
in the face with lock and chain.

The traumatized victim
tells the court she's terrified
to go outside, to ride the LRT,
to walk anywhere alone.

Jacking, robbery, theft
the impact on the victim
is the same,
as this young teen learns
when found guilty
of being party to the crime.

B & E

He won't tell who helped him,
says he didn't start the fire,
didn't see the smoke, just broke in,
entered a widow's house, broke
her windows, her locks, her heart,
looted her wedding band, her mother's jewelry.
Now she feels unsafe, violated, victimized.

He needed money for a toke,
shows no remorse, doesn't care
about the damage, her fears, her losses.
His mother thinks he needs boot camp.
She can't cope, doesn't want him
now he's broken, wants the courts to fix.

His fifteen-year-old limbs sprawl
all over the defendant's chair. He thinks
it all a joke, blames his father's death,
his attention disorder, the commute,
his mother, fear of his accomplice,
even blames the legal institute.
Blames everyone –
except himself.

The judge delays the sentencing,
wants to try another route,
wants the boy to meet his victim,
apologize, offer recompense, report
back in two months. Refers him
to people who will help. People
who believe that these young offenders
aren't really broken, just bent,
in need of some support
to grow straight again.

You Are Mother

Your daughter,
just fifteen, arrested
for soliciting,
on trial today.

You've never
been to court before,
find yourself alone
in the back row
not wanting to be noticed, hoping
the charges are false, hoping
that your daughter
will soon appear.

Courtroom whispers
weaken your resolve.
You want to be strong
for her, yet, alone
in this unfriendly place
doubts eat
holes in your courage.

You are mother
ready to plead guilty
to guilt,
guilty for loving,
guilty for feelings of failure,
guilty for the inability
to kiss it better
   any more.

How would he have pled?

He wasn't there in youth court Monday when they said his
     name.

He wasn't there when the charges were read.

He wasn't there to plead – guilty or not – to trafficking drugs.

He wasn't there to hear the prosecutor ask for dismissal instead.

He wasn't there when the judge asked why.

He wasn't there to hear, how last weekend –
he fled from the police,
hit another vehicle, slammed into a tree,
crack and cash strewn about his car.

He wasn't there when the case was dismissed.
            He wasn't there…

Outside Her Window

The girl in the prisoner's box
looks through her window,
sees a world outside so unlike the grays
of her own life lived in foster homes,
institutions, the street. A short while ago
the window opened to let in some colour –
she thought she was in love.
The man was her teacher, the only one
who'd ever paid attention, treated her
with kindness, made her feel special.
When the window slammed shut
she became obsessed, followed him, phoned him,
threatened to kill – him, his family, herself.
She was arrested, charged, confined.

Now she sits slumped forward, face hidden
by stringy hair while others speak;
severely depressed, sixteen, too old,
she can't go back, the teacher is there,
no place for her, no place outside her window,
no place in her ideal world of vibrant hues,
rose, citrine, amethyst, sapphire, amber, jade.

Betrayed at birth, betrayed by her first love,
betrayed again today as her future is tossed
back and forth like hot coals. The girl peeks
through her hair at the courtroom
that is so black and white, searching
for any window that will open
enough to allow her, at least,
to dream in colour.

Inferno

River rock, water has beaten you down, changed you.
This boy reaches for hair, sparks skin over bone.

Aspen, the air is still, why do you tremble?
This boy flickers in the courtroom.

Alien broom, you choke out the camas and the monkshood.
This boy tried to burn his father up.

Wind, your warnings scream through half-closed windows.
Almost man, this boy delights in sirens, engines, conflagration.

Colt, why gnaw your gate, the grass is tall and green beneath
        you.
This boy sings gasoline, matches to light up alleyways.

Flames in the hearth, you welcome us in from the cold.
This boy smoulders, asks for water, shelter, warmth.

Full moon, you've smiled down on us twice this month.
The boy sleeps, sedated, his hands extinguished.

The Hitch

There's no crease in his baggy jeans,
though the crotch reaches his knees
and his pant legs drag
over unlaced running shoes.
A grungy elbow pokes through
his sweatshirt as he stuffs thin hands
into back pockets and rocks
side to side taking a wide stance
in front of the judge who begins
to read his probation orders:
Keep the peace and be of good behavior.

He's fourteen, just pleaded guilty –
again to shoplifting. As he drops his head
dark clumps of hair fall forward
to cover pimples and a scowl
exposing scabby skin at the back
of his neck while shoulder wings jut
and flex, bony, featherless, grounded:
Keep the peace and be of good behavior.

A familiar phrase heard over
and over in youth court, but not
on the TV he watches, not in the music
he listens to, not in the movies he sees,
not on the streets where he's trying
to exist. Does this young man know
what that phrase means or,
are they just empty words to him:
Keep the peace and be of good behavior.

All he did was steal some food
because he was hungry. All he did
was run away from an abusive home.
All he did was get born
to a woman who didn't want
his kind of reminder around. How
can he possibly understand:
Keep the peace and be of good behavior.

It's a teasing echo in this courtroom.
If only it came with a recipe. If only
it could be bottled, could nourish
hungry youths like this one here
waiting for the judge's recitation to cease
before he's released, free to leave
with a hitch of those jeans, a scratch,
a timid grin and these words, which,
hopefully, he'll carry beyond these courtroom doors:
Keep the peace and be of good behavior.

Reprimanding the Boy in the Prisoner's Box

Stand up straight, sir.
I don't like you
leaning on the furniture.
You're only fourteen,
got yourself quite a record
already. Don't you see
what kind of a role model
you've been for your twelve-year-old brother,
stealing cars, breaking curfew and now
bringing guns into your mother's house.
What makes you do such things?
Peer pressure? Nonsense.
Get a backbone. Think for yourself.
Stop being a gutless follower.
Your mother tells me that
you do well in school –
when you try. Well, you'd better try
this time. If I had my way
I'd like to give you about four years
of custody, let you out when
you turned eighteen but I can't –
so it's 90 days closed custody,
45 days supervised plus one year
probation. I'd impose
a whole lot more –
if I could. Young man
your record is getting longer
and it's getting worse.
You'd better smarten up
if you don't want to spend
the rest of your life
        in a cage.

Marching Orders

– a found poem

You must	keep the peace	
You will	appear	
You can	not leave	
You must	report	
You will	provide	
You will	not use	
You will	be assessed	
You will	not possess	
You	will follow	
You	will take	
You	will tell	
You	will find	
You	will make	
You must	you will	you can
You must	you will	you can
Write	Apologize	Enroll
Write	Apologize	Enroll
You must	you will	
		You can!

FAMILY COURT

Between the Silences

It happens between the silences, amid whispers, flipping papers,
    coughs and bows.
It happens, they say, after previous consultation, and with due
    consideration.

It happens on paper in assessments, reports and addendums.
It happens between lawyers, social workers, judges.

Between the silences it happens; families are split, children
    discarded,
fathers and mothers appear and disappear, *the director* becomes
    parent.

It happens with grown-up words like: *custody, guardianship,*
    father unknown or absent,
mother served or signed release, supervision order, child in care,
    status extended.

It happens while children play in courthouse hallways.
A child's future determined in the time it takes to say:

So ordered.

Storm Warnings

In family court
on a blustery morning
in July, fifteen people
watch as a doctor speaks
and a judge listens
to determine the fate
of a three-year-old –
should her life be
spent with a mother
who still needs mothering
and a father
who has temper tantrums
or –
should she be set afloat
to drift aimlessly –
a foster child
in a stormy system.

Branded

Yesterday I overheard a lawyer
call a child *crack baby*
and I remembered my china doll
named Rosalee, wondered
if a newborn with such a label
could be assumed to be dispensable
as that broken doll.

Crack baby. Such a name
presumes hopelessness
for the baby who's been exposed
to drugs in the womb,
who's born addicted,
who meets withdrawal
rather than acceptance at birth.

Nobody really knows
what the future holds, for *crack babies*
are often victims by reputation
not actualization, starvation
not retardation, neglect
not brain damage.

Their biggest drawback –
their mothers
for they are the ones
really cracked.
If these children must
be labeled at all
let's call them –
>   *Children abused.*
>   *Children in trouble.*
>   *Children needing help.*

"I got my kid back, then I relapsed and they took her away again"

Her kid is five riding
an unmerry-go-round.
Up, she's with her mother,
down, she's with strangers,
up, down, round and round,
round and round in circles
of her mother's making,
alcohol, drugs, treatment –
      relapse.
Up, down, round and round.
Up, down, round and round.

Lady, lady, vow now,
face the music, make it stop,
take her off, stop the spinning,
help her stand on solid ground.
Up, down, round and round.
Up, down, round and round.
No more, no more making the rounds.

Your kid needs a mother
who will be there
for both her ups
    and
     her downs.

Alone and in Squalor

– found poem Edmonton Journal, Tues. June 8, 2004

Unfortunately
it happens often
three young brothers
left alone in a filthy apartment
the door open
the two little ones
playing in a puddle
the youngest one naked.

How hungry they were
chicken bones in a bowl.
The children's suite
reeked of urine and feces
a pig-sty of broken furniture
unwashed dishes, bare torn mattresses
sticky floors, dirty diapers
and on shelves high up
out of reach –
toys.

Over everything hung
a frilled blue oval sign:
Home Sweet Home.

The Week Before Christmas

Everything is stirring in youth court
as parents come to haggle
over who gets the children
during the holidays. There are no trees
or lights or tinsel here. Rank
antagonism decorates this courtroom.
All is not calm either
for muffled in the silences
is the racket of revenge.
Obstinate parents wanting
a judge to decide
who gets who for which days
and which times. Children
become bartering tools
as the where's
and when's
of the exchanges are set
amid hostile civility –
          civil hostility.

When all the children want
is to be nestled all snug in their beds.

When all the children want
is to sleep in heavenly peace.

Little Girl Lost

He brought her into the courtroom.
She wants to take her home.

Four-year-old Maggie plays
around their feet where they stand
at opposing counsel tables
telling the judge their sides.
Voices angry, bodies tense
they list the reasons why
they can't agree on custody.

The little girl crawls out
from under the tables,
takes Daddy's hand
then reaches across
that hostile space
to grab Mommy's hand
and hangs there lost
in the uncertainty
of the in-between.

There Was a Young Woman

This woman isn't old, doesn't live in a shoe,
but she's had nine babies – hasn't kept one.
Says their father's on drugs, her life
too unsettled, someone/anyone else
will do a better job, better for her
to make the sacrifice.

In court she calmly explains
her reasons for giving up
custody of her newest born
daughter to the couple already
raising her two-year-old son.

She's well groomed, attractive,
still quite young, pragmatic but polite
as she recites her situation to the judge,
proud to be able to help, wants her children
to be happy and no –
she won't be asking for them back.

So permanent guardianship is granted.
She doesn't seem bothered, in fact,
perhaps pleased that she's done such
a good deed for this couple's family.

Picking up purse, scarf and gloves
she leaves the courtroom without
hesitation. Having abdicated
motherhood again, one cannot help
but wonder just when she'll be returning
to give up number ten.

.

she said:

he said

I'm being denied access

I need to be with my children

I'm being defamed

I'm not a bad mother

I need to speak

it's been months

I'm not schizophrenic

he gambles

I was depressed

lost our house

drank a lot

he's violent

took drugs

I'm afraid

hit her only once

need a restraining order

knocked her down

we're separated

I was sorry

he's addicted to VLT's

cried about that

they took my kids away

went through rehab

can't afford a lawyer

have a job

want my kids back

don't want to see a psychiatrist

she's the one who's crazy

Custody & Access

Once it was all about love,
simple, for this man and woman,
then along came three children,
too soon, too many, things went wrong,
they bickered, they brawled until finally he left.
She still waits for him to come back.

He swears he's not going back.
He's found a new love,
outlines the problems, why he left,
couldn't stay with this woman,
but admits it was wrong
to abandon his children.

He's worried about the children,
testifies she lies behind his back,
now they're scared of him. That's wrong.
He just wants them living where there's love,
not ignored or neglected by a woman
still nasty and bitter as when he first left.

Three years since he left,
three years away from his children,
three years divorced, yet this woman,
still focused on getting him back,
has no time for her own kids, no love
either, doesn't understand what went wrong.

She's unable to tell right from wrong,
a head injury ten years ago left
her childlike, searching for love,
not able to care for her own children.
Now their father seeks custody and she cannot back
up her claim, cannot comprehend he has another woman.

The judge listens to this unfortunate woman
who won't accept that it is wrong
to presume this man is coming back.
She vows she'll kill herself if left
alone, renounce her own children,
cut off her absent love.

This woman still hungers for the love of this man.
Her children have suffered too long for this wrong,
have been left believing their dad's still coming back.

Hindsight

they were blind   they were blind   the three now standing in
the aisle of the courtroom   mother father   stepfather   they
just didn't see   blinded by her beauty   such a lovely baby   cute
toddler   adorable child   they gave her everything   gave into her
everythings   she was so nice   you should have seen how they ran
the sacrifice   you should have seen   how they ran when she cried
how they ran to make their petite towheaded girl happy   now
their sweet little girl is grown up   has a mind of her own   a drug
vice & a boyfriend who's not very nice   jailed twice   so they all run
after their little girl to the boyfriend's house where she threatens
them with a knife   they'd never seen such anger   her defiance
her malice her rage   sliced open their blindness   their lovable
daughter   now a sick angry young woman   locked up so she
can do no more harm   in the prisoner's box she remains defiant
despite her stepfather's sighs   her father's pleas   her mother's
sobs   the judge's advice   says she'll do as she pleases   did you
ever see such a sight in your life as those three   no longer blind
now they see clearly her plight under this courtroom's bright light
now they see   now they see

Blessed are these

mothers who, having already raised one
family are prepared to start over
with their children's children,
willing to pick up the pieces
of those young lives, to try
to repair the damage already done
through neglect or abuse.
It can't be easy when one is older
to cope with the vitality,
the demands of the young.

These women are grand-
mothers, truly grand-grandmothers
who come to court,
dedicate themselves anew,
publicly pledge to take on
all the obligations required
to raise yet another child –
or two or even more sometimes –
because their own adult child
can no longer parent.

Drugs, alcohol, separation, work, money,
disinterest, divorce, disease, death –
so many reasons,
so many needy children
and far too few of these
grand-grandmothers.

One Mother's Plight

The first time he took the baby
she came back with a diaper rash,
the second visit, a small cut
over her eye, the third time
she crawled into a plastic bag,
inhaled cement dust, had to be
hospitalized. Every second Saturday
she has to let this man who fathered
her child have access, has to let him
take her baby away for a visit, unsupervised –
because he is living with his parents but –
she tells the court, they're never there.
She's worried, doesn't want
this man left alone with her precious
six month old, says the baby cries,
clings to her whenever he comes
around, says she has to peel
her frightened daughter off,
hand her screaming to this man
every second week, says he's mean,
has a temper, used to hit her.

I'm afraid, she tells the judge
wiping away her tears, *afraid*
that if my baby cries too much
he'll get mad, I'm afraid
he'll shake her. I'm afraid for my baby.
I know that he doesn't really care,
he's just mad at me for going to court,
for making him pay. Now
he says he'll make me pay.
Please do something –
I'm so afraid.

D~I~V~O~R~C~E

Death doesn't always do the parting
       desk divorce is another way to go
         an office rend

Ideally done between lawyer and judge
       irreconcilable differences inferred
         no corpus delicti

Visions of one happy family vanish
       validated by vague recriminations
         it's hipper to be civ

Oppressive circumstances
       often money is mistress
       adultery also

Regrets come later
       riding a lonely trail
         bridled in anger

Cohabitation impossible
       courtesy the cue to closure
        a polite tactic

Everyone pays
       especially the children
         a significant consequence

Dads' Daze In Court

This dad's frustrated,
wants his kid back, doesn't have
a lawyer, didn't apply
for legal aid, doesn't even
have a place to live. Tells the judge
he's fed up "with all this shit."
He's too busy to come to court,
doesn't have time to get a lawyer,
wants his kid back, thinks he can
look after him, plug him in anywhere,
just like his cell phone now charging
in the back row of the courtroom.

*

This dad's angry
at the child welfare worker.
His daughter is two years old today,
has been in care for two years
less one day. Now her foster parents
want to adopt. His wife is mentally ill,
won't leave the house to see their child,
doesn't want her husband to leave either.
He keeps missing visits, upsets the child,
has only seen her three times altogether. Now
he wants to fight the permanent guardianship
order, still thinks that someday his wife
will be better, someday he will be a good father,
someday…

*

This dad's worried
that he will never
see his son again
if his mother is allowed
to take him back
to visit her family
in Trinidad.

*

This dad refuses
to go to mediation, states
he and his ex-wife cannot agree
on anything, each stubbornly stuck
on what they want, while
the concerns of their child fade
into the smoke of their vengeance.

*

This dad's scared
for his daughter. Her
mother is an alcoholic,
takes drugs, has left
the child before,
in movie theatres, stores, cars
outside of bars. Now she stands
unsteadily to ask the court's permission
for an overnight visit, promises
to take a blood test to prove
she's clean. He wipes at tears,
fearfully protests, wants only the best
for this five-year-old girl
he's raised since birth.

*

This dad's shocked,
the mother of his five-year-old son
has just accused his fiancée's
son, aged ten, of sexual
molestation. He doesn't
believe it, suggests perhaps
his son made up the story
prompted by his mother
now that he's engaged
to another woman.

*

This dad's disturbed
to hear his teenage son
testify to being part of the group
who threatened and harassed
a younger boy, disturbed
to realize his son
is a bully.

*

This dad's distressed
his four year old son gone
to Italy on vacation
with his mother
hasn't come back, has gone
into hiding, gone
out of his life, gone,
and he doesn't know
what to do.

*

This dad's on parole
for murder, seeks custody
of his five-year-old daughter
now that her mother has gone to jail.

*

This dad denies
the accusation that he drank
and smoked pot with his children,
wants the judge to enforce
his access order even though
his children don't want
to see him any more.

*

This dad just woke up,
now he wants custody
of the two-year-old boy
he fathered but never saw,
never supported, never
cared about, until –
his mother applied
for sole custody.

*

This dad's afraid
of his seventeen-year-old son
tells the court that drugs
have changed him, now
he's threatening his mother,
his sister, himself, wants
an order to have him
arrested, assessed and assisted.

*

This dad's fighting
for custody of one of his two
BMW Z8 convertibles,
says they go too fast, he's worried
about the safety of his ex-wife,
his children, would rather give her
one of his four trucks.

*

This dad's happy
to apply for custody
of his son after seven years.
In court they sit close
together playing X's and O's
waiting their turn.

*

This dad's agitated,
believes his mentally challenged
son is being neglected. He doesn't
have custody, hasn't been in touch
for years. Now he says
nobody will listen, nobody
understands. His speech get louder
as he issues his demands to the judge,
protesting righteously that he must do this
for his son even if it means
he will be escorted from the courtroom
one more time.

*

This dad denies paternity,
doesn't want to pay,
not even for the DNA test,
says he wasn't
the only one.

WITH DUE CARE AND ATTENTION

The Judge's Robe

No ceremony that to great ones 'long,
Not the king's crown, nor the deputed sword,
The marshal's truncheon, nor the judge's robe
Become them with one half so good a grace
As mercy does.
— Measure for Measure, *William Shakespeare*

It seems as if judges are about to take flight
when they swoop into the courtroom,
their black robes winging out in all directions,
white tabs under chins unruly as feathers.
We stand when they enter, sit after they've
settled on the dais. Not by their song,
no, these birds are identified by their trim. Perched
above the rest of the courtroom their presence commands
respect, for the privilege of the robe is strong
though *no ceremony that to great ones belong*

can be taken lightly. It is to that robe that people bow,
hats are removed, oaths are taken and lawyers ask
permission to speak. It is from that robe that we seek direction.
It's a heavy mantle, for the people who wear it
are the ones who must decide, alone, with the law
as their measure. If a shared humanity is to be restored
there must be room enough inside that gown for the tools
needed for the job; humility, integrity, empathy, knowledge,
humor. For there's power in a judge's robe which strikes a chord
even though it's *not the king's crown nor the deputed sword,*

it's just as weighty, especially when the young are at risk.
Children whose parents are children themselves. Children
ignored, battered and abused. Teenage boys who fight
with knives and guns, girls who bully, youths who steal cars,
rob to feed drug habits, troubled young people setting fires,
babies abandoned and a young woman with a torn ear lobe
and a broken nose wanting police protection from her husband.
They all come to seek help from the robe believing that
the person inside can work miracles. But if you were to probe
you'd find neither *the marshal's truncheon, nor the judge's robe*

is omnipotent. Underneath there lives a human being,
male, female, son, daughter, husband, wife,
parent, grandparent, friend. Underneath they carry
their own insecurities, flaws and scars.
Underneath they're just ordinary people
doing an extraordinary job trying with each case
to be fair and just. Believing in our justice system
they don their gowns and pretend that they can fly because
they know the magic of a judge's robe is in the ordinary trace
and even that doesn't *become them with one half so good a grace*
— as mercy does.

At the Preliminary Murder Trial

One man is dead,
another accused of murder,
yet the victim's wife seems more concerned
about her hair and lipstick
as she takes the stand
to testify about that day;
how she watched it all
through her rear view mirror, how she
took off her seatbelt to light a cigarette
just before she heard the shot,
saw her husband fall, heard his scream,
saw the accused roll up the car window
and – speed away.

The accused listens,
tips his chair back, yawns
and surreptitiously smirks
at his friends from his seat
in the prisoners box.

A father is dead at twenty-one
and his child's cry seeps
through the courtroom doors
cranky with the why of it all.

Application for Mental Health Warrant

It's hard, he says, *so hard*.
A middle-aged man,
grey haired and rotund wipes
at tears behind thick glasses
takes the warrant
from the judge, his wife's
apprehension. Ten years,
he tells the court, ten years
of curtains closed, unanswered
calls, friends turned away.
Ten years of silence,
of anger, of hearing voices,
checking for wires
and microphones. Once
she was outgoing, active and happy, now
she won't leave the house, won't
see a doctor, refuses to take
her medication. Yesterday
she threatened to throw boiling
water over him. He's worried
for her, not sure what he'd do
if she grabbed a knife –

This is hard, he says,
his voice breaking,
so very hard.

He takes the warrant, wants
to wait, wants
to talk to her again, wants
the police to be kind, wants
back his wife
of forty years.

Pleas

Your honor, my father needs help,
he's living in his car, thinks
the police are after him
with a taser gun, thinks
his apartment is bugged,
he's mentally ill, refuses
to see a doctor, to take
his medications, scares
my children, threatens
my Mom, my sister,
he needs help,
we need help,
we don't know
where else
to go, please
help us, help
him, he
won't last
the winter,
he'll freeze,
he's seventy-two,
old
and scared
and sick,
help
please
help
us,
help
him
p
l
e
a
s

e.

The Toughest Kind of Love

But, he's really not a bad man, his mother said.
It's just lately he's got confused.
They were a simple, honest couple,
They'd never been to court before.

It's just lately he's got confused.
The police told them it was the only way.
They'd never been to court before,
yet they came, reluctant parents.

The police told them it was the only way.
Loath to tell the judge anything bad about their son,
yet they came, reluctant parents
finally confessing under oath that he abuses them.

Loath to tell the judge anything bad about their son,
how he shoves them around, takes their money,
finally confessing under oath that he abuses them.
They just want him to leave them alone.

How he shoves them around, takes their money.
They are a simple, honest couple.
They just want him to leave them alone.
But, he's really not a bad man, his mother said.

Ex parte

At the end of the morning in Courtroom 442
a frail woman smoothes her skirt
looks around furtively through one black eye
as she limps to the stand, holds the Bible
between quivering hands and takes a vow
to tell the truth – *so help me God.*

Her voice quivers. She left her husband
yesterday, is hiding in a safe house now,
doesn't feel safe, wants her husband
to stay away, he's doing drugs, beats her
up, threatens her mother, her brother.

The judge writes an emergency
protection order. Her husband
is to leave her alone, a policeman
will escort her home to pick up her belongings.

She takes the order, scurries from the courtroom.

Safe?

Protected?

So help me God!

Glossary of Court Terms

B & E (breaking and entry): term used to describe the necessary elements of a burglary which consists of breaking and entering a dwelling to commit an offence.

Community service: a criminal sentence requiring that the offender perform some specific service to the community for some specified period of time.

Custody: this term is very elastic and may mean actual imprisonment or physical detention or mere power, legal or physical, of imprisoning or, of taking manual possession.

Custody of children: the care, control and maintenance of a child which may be awarded by a court to one of the parents as in a divorce or separation proceeding.

Defendant: the person defending or denying; the accused in a criminal case.

Ex parte: where one side can apply without the other side being present.

Guardianship: a legal arrangement under which one person (a guardian) has the legal right and duty to care for another (the ward) and his or her property.

Mental Health Warrant: an order of the Court allowing a person to be arrested and placed in a psychiatric facility for a fixed period of time to be assessed.

Party to the crime: a co-defendant; one among several charged with the same crime.

Probation: sentence imposed for commission of crime whereby a convicted criminal offender is released into the community under the supervision of a probation officer in lieu of incarceration.

Prisoner: one who is kept against his will in confinement or custody in a prison, or other correctional institution as a result of conviction of a crime or while awaiting trial.

The Director: in this case refers to the Director of Child Welfare.

Trafficking: trading or dealing in certain goods; commonly used in connection with illegal narcotic sales.

Young Offender: a youth under the age of 18 years who has been charged with a criminal offence.

Youth docket court: where young offenders make their first appearance to enter their plea and get a trial date or receive a sentence.

Ward of the Court: infants or persons of unsound mind placed by the court under the care of a guardian.

Witness: a person whose declaration under oath is received as evidence for any purpose, whether such declaration be made on oral examination or by deposition or affidavit.

Diane Buchanan is a poet and essayist who has lived in and around Edmonton, Alberta all her life. The last thirty years have been spent on a thoroughbred horse farm where she and her husband of forty-three years raised four daughters. She began to write after retiring from nursing and returning to University at the age of fifty. Her first book of poetry, *Ask Her Anything*, was published in 2001.